Trends in Southeast Asia

2015   #04

Trends in Southeast Asia

EXPLAINING CHINA'S
2+7 INITIATIVE TOWARDS ASEAN

DAVID ARASE

ISEAS Publishing
INSTITUTE OF SOUTHEAST ASIAN STUDIES

Published by: ISEAS Publishing
                 Institute of Southeast Asian Studies
                 30 Heng Mui Keng Terrace
                 Pasir Panjang, Singapore 119614
                 publish@iseas.edu.sg http://bookshop.iseas.edu.sg

ISEAS Library Cataloguing-in-Publication Data

Arase, David.
    Explaining China's 2+7 Initiative towards ASEAN.
    (Trends in Southeast Asia, 0219-3213 ; TRS 4/15)
    1. China—Foreign relations—21st century.
    2. Economic assistance, Chinese—Southeast Asia.
    3. Investments, Chinese—Southeast Asia.
    4. South China Sea—International status.
    5. Southeast Asia—Foreign relations—China.
    6. China—Foreign relations—Southeast Asia.
    I. Title.
    II. Series: Trends in Southeast Asia ; TRS 4/15.
DS501 I59T no. 4(2015)   2015

ISBN 978-981-4620-78-9 (soft cover)
ISBN 978-981-4620-79-6 (e-book, PDF)

Typeset by Superskill Graphics Pte Ltd
Printed in Singapore by Mainland Press Pte Ltd

FOREWORD

The economic, political, strategic and cultural dynamism in Southeast Asia has gained added relevance in recent years with the spectacular rise of giant economies in East and South Asia. This has drawn greater attention to the region and to the enhanced role it now plays in international relations and global economics.

The sustained effort made by Southeast Asian nations since 1967 towards a peaceful and gradual integration of their economies has had indubitable success, and perhaps as a consequence of this, most of these countries are undergoing deep political and social changes domestically and are constructing innovative solutions to meet new international challenges. Big Power tensions continue to be played out in the neighbourhood despite the tradition of neutrality exercised by the Association of Southeast Asian Nations (ASEAN).

The **Trends in Southeast Asia** series acts as a platform for serious analyses by selected authors who are experts in their fields. It is aimed at encouraging policy makers and scholars to contemplate the diversity and dynamism of this exciting region.

THE EDITORS

Series Chairman:
    Tan Chin Tiong

Series Editors:
    Su-Ann Oh
    Ooi Kee Beng
    Terence Chong

Editorial Committee:
    Francis E. Hutchinson
    Daljit Singh

Explaining China's 2+7 Initiative Towards ASEAN

By David Arase

EXECUTIVE SUMMARY

- China's 2+7 Initiative towards ASEAN aims to create an economic, security and political partnership that will be deeper than ASEAN's partnerships with other external powers.
- This partnership would be inherently unequal and China's effort to secure this relationship should be seen in the context of China's agenda to achieve great power status. China seeks Southeast Asian followers within a larger China-centred Eurasian community.
- The 2+7 Initiative diverts attention from South China Sea territorial disputes and directs the attention of ASEAN as a whole towards new Chinese aid, trade, and investment. In exchange for economic resources, China hopes to establish new common understandings in the management of Southeast Asian political and security affairs.
- China's agenda could inhibit ASEAN's freedom and centrality in regional agenda-setting. And a new political-security partnership with China that ignored its unilateral coercive efforts to change the territorial status quo in the South China Sea would accept and normalize a situation that worked against important national interests of certain ASEAN members.
- To succeed in its effort to develop greater institutional strength and unity, ASEAN must pay attention to the distribution of costs and benefits that agreements with external powers generate. To guard its unity and integrity, ASEAN should agree that it will not sacrifice the interests of some members in order to gain benefits for others.

Explaining China's 2+7 Initiative Towards ASEAN

By David Arase[1]

INTRODUCTION

China's 2+7 Initiative towards ASEAN was first advanced by Premier Li Keqiang at the October 2013 China-ASEAN summit, and he reaffirmed it at the November 2014 China-ASEAN summit.[2] This 2+7 Initiative uses economic incentives to raise formal policy dialogue and coordination in regional economic, political, and security matters between China and ASEAN to a higher level than ASEAN presently enjoys with any other dialogue partner. This initiative is the product of China's new agenda under the leadership of President Xi Jinping to achieve great power status.

What will it mean for ASEAN? To answer this question, I first review the 2+7 initiative and then proceed to indicate how it reflects Xi Jinping's broader agenda to achieve the "great rejuvenation of the Chinese nation," the ultimate rhetorical aim of Xi Jinping's leadership agenda which will be explained in more detail below. Next, I discuss the trade-offs created

---

[1] Professor David Arase was a Visiting Senior Fellow at ISEAS. He is a Resident Professor of International Politics at The Hopkins-Nanjing Center for Chinese and American Studies at Nanjing University, The Johns Hopkins-School of Advanced International Studies (SAIS).

[2] Remarks by H.E. Li Keqiang Premier of the State Council of the People's Republic of China At the 16th ASEAN-China Summit, 10 October 2013 <http://www.fmprc.gov.cn/mfa_eng/topics_665678/lkqzlcxdyldrxlhy_665684/t1089853.shtml>; Remarks by H.E. Li Keqiang Premier of the State Council of the People's Republic of China At the 17th ASEAN-China Summit, 13 November 2014 <http://www.fmprc.gov.cn/mfa_eng/wjb_663304/zzjg_663340/yzs_663350/xwlb_663352/t1212266.shtml>.

1

by China's diplomatic initiative. I conclude with thoughts about how ASEAN can deal with external powers that offer cooperation packages such as the 2+7 Initiative.

CHINA'S NEW DIPLOMATIC INITIATIVE TOWARDS ASEAN

In March 2013, the National Peoples' Congress elected Xi Jinping as President (head of state) and Li Keqiang as Premier (head of government) of China. At that moment, China's relations with ASEAN not only lacked forward momentum, but were vexed by discord caused by assertive unilateral Chinese actions since 2009 to advance control over its ill-defined 9-dash line jurisdictional claim in the South China Sea.

China's new leaders wasted little time in lifting China-ASEAN relations out of the doldrums. Premier Li Keqiang and President Xi Jinping made separate visits to Southeast Asia in October 2013, but the two visits were coordinated to lay out an ambitious vision for the future of China-ASEAN cooperative relations. Premier Li Keqiang proposed a concrete cooperation agenda called the "2+7 Initiative" at the 2013 China-ASEAN Summit.[3] The goal is to advance policy coordination in two broad areas simultaneously: regional security-political policy coordination and regional economic development. To advance cooperation in both areas, Li Keqiang offered seven policy agendas to be outlined below.

President Xi made a more visionary call for China-ASEAN partnership during his visits to Indonesia and Malaysia. He proposed the establishment of a new Asian Infrastructure Investment Bank and announced a "21st Century Maritime Silk Road" initiative to boost China-ASEAN maritime cooperation and trade through Chinese investment in port infrastructure development.[4] Xi Jinping also spoke of his desire

---

[3] Ibid.

[4] Creating a New Landscape for the Diplomacy with Neighboring Countries and Boosting the Asia-Pacific Regional Cooperation — Foreign Minister Wang Yi Talks about President Xi Jinping's Visit to Indonesia and Malaysia and Attendance of the 21st APEC Economic Leaders' Meeting. 9 October 2013 <http://www.fmprc.gov.cn/mfa_eng/wjb_663304/wjbz_663308/2461_663310/t1088099.shtml>.

to unite China and ASEAN into a "Community of Common Destiny" (*mingyun gongtongti*).[5] The vision that Xi Jinping painted is both new and central to China's approach to ASEAN, but it is not exclusive to ASEAN. That is, the proposed institutions, norms, and agreements that Xi alluded to when he mentioned the 21st Century Maritime Silk Road, the Asian Infrastructure Development Bank, and the Community of Common Destiny include countries outside of Southeast Asia because these proposals, discussed below, help to constitute China's overall Eurasian agenda as a great power.

What is new, central, and *specific* to ASEAN is Li Keqiang's 2+7 Initiative, and so we will focus on this before moving on to consider how it fits into the broader great power vision of China.

The 2+7 Initiative

In his speech at the 2013 ASEAN-China summit, Li Keqiang offered two fundamental principles, i.e., political-security cooperation and economic cooperation, to be developed in tandem as the basis of China-ASEAN relations. He then proposed seven negotiation agendas that advance China-ASEAN relations on both fronts:

1. sign a new China-ASEAN treaty of good neighbourliness and cooperation;
2. begin an annual China-ASEAN defence ministers' meeting;
3. upgrade the ASEAN-China FTA and reach US$1 trillion in two-way trade by 2020;
4. create a new Asian Infrastructure Investment Bank;
5. expand renminbi (RMB) currency swaps, RMB trade invoicing, and RMB banking services;
6. build maritime cooperation in the South China Sea via, among other things, an annual maritime ministerial meeting; and

---

[5] China vows to build community of common destiny with ASEAN, Xinhuanet, 3 October 2013 <news.xinhuanet.com/english/china/2013-10/03/c_132770494. htm>.

7. promote cultural exchange, scientific, and environmental cooperation.[6]

The first two agenda items (the China-ASEAN treaty of good neighbourliness and cooperation; and the annual China-ASEAN defence ministers' meeting) advance the political-security cooperation principle. The rest advance the economic cooperation principle but they are not devoid of political and security implications. However, what is missing is any offer of an olive branch over the South China Sea problem. On the contrary, Premier Li stated that, "The Chinese government is … unshakable in its resolve to uphold national sovereignty and territorial integrity."[7]

At the next ASEAN-China summit meeting in December 2014, Li reaffirmed Xi Jinping's visionary agenda and his own 2+7 initiative offered the previous year.[8] With respect to the seven negotiation agendas he proposed in 2013, Li pointed to specific achievements in points 3, 4, and 7 listed above, namely, negotiations to upgrade the China-ASEAN FTA (point 3); a signed agreement to establish the AIIB (point 4); and formation of the Network of ASEAN-China Think Tanks as well as other human exchange programmes (point 7). Li could point to no solid advances in the political-security policy coordination, but China expects progress here to match progress in economic cooperation. The conflicting claims over island ownership and/or maritime jurisdictional rights in the South China Sea involving China, Vietnam, the Philippines,

---

[6] Remarks by H.E. Li Keqiang Premier of the State Council of the People's Republic of China At the 16th ASEAN-China Summit, 10 October 2013. <http://www.fmprc.gov.cn/mfa_eng/topics_665678/lkqzlcxdyldrxlhy_665684/t1089853.shtml>.

[7] "China-ASEAN relationship still thrives", Chinadaily.com, 9 October 2013 <http://usa.chinadaily.com.cn/china/2013-10/09/content_17015977_2.htm>.

[8] Remarks by H.E. Li Keqiang Premier of the State Council of the People's Republic of China At the 17th ASEAN-China Summit, 13 November 2014 <http://www.fmprc.gov.cn/mfa_eng/wjb_663304/zzjg_663340/yzs_663350/xwlb_663352/t1212266.shtml>.

Brunei, Malaysia, Indonesia and Taiwan explain this lack of progress, and the relationship of this question to the 2+7 initiative will be discussed after looking at the details of the 2+7 initiative.

What China Offers

China offers ASEAN countries a substantial list of material inducements to advance its 2+7 initiative. This list includes: US$10 billion in concessional China-ASEAN project loans; RMB50 million in grants for ASEAN community building; RMB3 billion in development grants to the less developed countries of Indochina (Cambodia, Laos, Myanmar and Vietnam); RMB30 million to promote enhancement of the China-ASEAN FTA; a second phase replenishment of the China-ASEAN Investment Cooperation Fund of US$3 billion; a US$10 billion special loan by the China Development Bank for China-ASEAN infrastructure development to be implemented by Chinese firms relocating to Southeast Asia; and a China-ASEAN Maritime Cooperation Fund to finance maritime cooperation activities.[9]

China also offers ASEAN members cooperative political and technical support in a variety of ways. Examples include a new Mekong River dialogue and cooperation mechanism; support for poverty reduction; construction of trans-border economic cooperation zones and industrial parks; research and cooperation in harmonizing trade and financial procedures; planning for enhanced connectivity in transportation, telecommunications, power, and the internet; sponsorship of a China-ASEAN maritime cooperation centre; a ministerial level maritime cooperation forum; the Pan-Beibu Gulf Economic Cooperation Action Roadmap; disaster management cooperation; construction of China-ASEAN Education and Training Centres; agricultural technology

---

[9] Remarks by H.E. Li Keqiang Premier of the State Council of the People's Republic of China At the 17th ASEAN-China Summit, 13 November 2014 <http://www.fmprc.gov.cn/mfa_eng/wjb_663304/zzjg_663340/yzs_663350/xwlb_663352/t1212266.shtml>; "News Analysis: China, ASEAN embarking on cooperation of 'diamond decade'," Xinhuanet, 11 November 2014 <http://news.xinhuanet.com/english/indepth/2014-11/11/c_133781595.htm>.

demonstration centres; and technical, scientific, and educational exchange programmes.[10]

What China Expects

Winning ASEAN followership not only realizes China's ambition for great power status; it also gives China "face" that translates into domestic political legitimacy for Beijing. The idea is to use economic incentives to lead ASEAN into broader and deeper "all-dimensional" cooperation. By cultivating ASEAN economic dependence China gains privileged institutionalized access and greater leverage among ASEAN members. Those members most dependent on China may be tempted to trade their influence inside ASEAN to gain additional benefits from China. The result would be ASEAN policies and activities that avoid relations with other powers that might displease China. An ASEAN that respected China's core interests and great power ambitions above all else would constitute a harmonious and prosperous Asian community under Chinese leadership.

Though ASEAN agreement to new security cooperation with China—even as China continues to disrupt the territorial status quo in the South China Sea—may signal acceptance of China's behaviour and 9-dash line territorial and jurisdictional claims, to ASEAN members such as Thailand, Laos, Cambodia, and Myanmar with no territorial claims or maritime resources at stake in the South China Sea, the material inducements that China offers to move this new security cooperation agenda forward may be persuasive.

The South China Sea Question and the 2+7 Initiative

The reason for lagging political-security cooperation in the 2+7 Initiative is China's harsh South China Sea maritime confrontations with Vietnam and the Philippines; its refusal to acknowledge the authority of impartial international adjudicatory mechanisms under international law to resolve

---

[10] Ibid.

land and maritime jurisdictional disputes connected to China's 9-dash line claim; stalled talks between China and ASEAN over a legally binding Code of Conduct in the South China Sea; and China's methodical, incremental and unilateral actions to change the maritime status quo at the expense of rival claimants' sovereignty claims, e.g., at Scarborough Shoal/Huangyandao in 2012,[11] Chinese province Hainan's declared intention to enforce exclusive fishing rights in two million km^2 of the South China Sea,[12] and the construction of new artificial dual-use islands in contested areas.[13] These behaviours suggest an uncompromising Chinese claim to exclusive jurisdiction within the 9-dash line.

When acting unilaterally to secure exclusive control within its 9-dash line claim, China relies primarily on paramilitary forces, i.e., its fishing fleets, maritime safety, and civilian maritime law enforcement agencies. It has bigger and more numerous civilian patrol vessels than rival claimants, and they are regularly used to defend Chinese vessels operating in disputed waters and chase away or arrest non-Chinese vessels operating inside China's 9-dash line. Were China to use military force for this purpose, rival claimants could call it military aggression. China might call it defensive action but to initiate military conflict would harm China's international image. Therefore, China relies on civilian force to advance control below the threshold of military conflict. If outclassed rival claimants resort to military force to resist the civilian Chinese advance, China has at hand superior military force to "defend" its territorial integrity and national sovereignty. This formula ensures that the expansion of Chinese control remains both successful and "peaceful".

---

[11] Nguyen Manh Hung, "ASEAN's Scarborough Failure?", *The Diplomat*, 16 June 2012 <http://thediplomat.com/2012/06/aseans-scarborough-failure/>. "Q&A: South China Sea dispute," BBC News, 8 May 2014 <http://www.bbc.com/news/world-asia-pacific-13748349>.

[12] "The South China Sea: Hai-handed—China creates an ADIZ for fish", *The Economist*, 18 January 2014 <http://www.economist.com/news/asia/21594355-china-creates-adiz-fish-hai-handed>.

[13] "China Expands Island Construction in Disputed South China Sea," *Wall Street Journal*, 18 February 2015 <http://www.wsj.com/articles/china-expands-island-construction-in-disputed-south-china-sea-1424290852>.

A key Chinese assumption is that this paramilitary maritime campaign can continue without obstructing new political-security cooperation with ASEAN under the 2+7 Initiative. Premier Li stated that, "Though there exist disputes between China and some ASEAN countries regarding the South China Sea, this does not affect overall stability in the South China Sea, and freedom and safety of navigation in the South China Sea is guaranteed." China will discuss overall peace and security in the South China Sea so long as its maritime disputes with ASEAN members are not a topic. China argues that the disputes do not directly concern every ASEAN member so China will not discuss its disputes with ASEAN as a whole. To deal with its disputes with ASEAN members, China offers only a bilateral negotiation with each individual claimant country as a path to legal resolution. Premier Li stated in his speech, "Specific disputes are to be addressed by countries directly concerned peacefully through negotiation and consultation based on historical facts, international law and the DOC..."[14]

This "dual track approach" ensures that these disputes will not become the subject of discussion between China and ASEAN as a whole and it forecloses legal resolution of disputes by appeal to independent and impartial international judicial mechanisms.[15]

China agreed in July 2013 to talk with ASEAN about a COC that would set legally binding good behaviour rules pending resolution of the conflicts. Progress in the infrequent rounds of COC talks is hard to detect. In a bid to speed the agreement, in February 2015 Malaysia proposed to discuss the COC at the ASEAN Defence Ministers' Meeting Plus to be held in November, but China rejected the proposal.[16] China

---

[14] Remarks by H.E. Li Keqiang Premier of the State Council of the People's Republic of China At the 17th ASEAN-China Summit, 13 November 2014. Ibid.

[15] "Li vows S.China Sea stability", *Sina English*, 14 November 2014 <http://english.sina.com/china/p/2014/1113/754340.html>; "FM rejects South China Sea arbitration", *Global Times*, 8 December 2015 <http://www.globaltimes.cn/content/895453.shtml>.

[16] "South China Sea issues blunt progress at ADSOM Plus", HIS Jane's 360, 16 February 2015 <http://www.janes.com/article/49009/south-china-sea-issues-

hopes to contain ASEAN objections to Chinese activity in the South China Sea inside the special purpose COC talks so they do not attach to, and obstruct, China's 2+7 initiative.

Premier Li proposed in the 2014 ASEAN-China meeting that, "peace and security of the South China Sea be jointly upheld by China and ASEAN countries working together." This proposed basis for security cooperation needs critical examination. Peace and security in the South China Sea is not an exclusive responsibility arrogated by China with the cooperation or permission of ASEAN. The right of all states to safety and freedom in the South China Sea is established under international law, is justiciable using impartial legal procedures and authorities, and it concerns the entire international community.

ASEAN should take care that its interest in upholding the open global commons and the international rule of law is reflected in any political-security agreements that it undertakes with an external power, especially if that power seeks a dominant hand in managing Southeast Asian security.

Strategic Tradeoffs and Consequences

In order to speed the 2+7 initiative forward, China wants its South China Sea disputes with ASEAN members disconnected from the collective ASEAN agenda and side-tracked into the China-ASEAN COC talks about rules of behaviour, or into bilateral negotiations between China and individual rival claimants to find final legal resolution. The 2+7 Initiative contains substantial economic rewards not only for side-tracking the South China Sea dispute, but also for advancing new regional political-security cooperation with China across a broad front. However, for ASEAN to advance closer political-security policy coordination of the sort China proposes—even as China acts to erode the sovereign rights

---

blunt-progress-at-adsom-plus>; "Deep divisions keep South China Sea issues off Asean agenda", *South China Morning Post*, 2 March 2015 <http://www.scmp.com/comment/insight-opinion/article/1727672/deep-divisions-keep-south-china-sea-issues-asean-agenda>.

claimed by ASEAN members such as Vietnam and the Philippines—
would effectively acquiesce to China's behaviour and 9-dash line
claim. Moreover, any agreement that prevents ASEAN from expressing
a collective viewpoint on the South China Sea disputes would render
implausible the whole idea of ASEAN centrality in the construction of
regional norms and institutions governing peace and security in Southeast
Asia.

Premier Li urged ASEAN to side-track the South China Sea dispute
and move ahead with the 2+7 Initiative by saying, "Our shared interests
and the affinity of our cultural tradition far outweigh our different views
and disagreements."[17] Later, when deeper economic dependence on
China gives it increased leverage, individual ASEAN claimants may feel
more compelled to renounce their sovereign legal rights as coastal states
under the United Nations Convention on the Law of the SEA (UNCLOS)
in favour of China's historical claims.

However, if China miscalculates ASEAN's response and the South
China Sea controversy remains visible in headlines, this could rouse
anti-Chinese nationalism in Southeast Asia, alienate world opinion, keep
alive the risk of local conflicts and external intervention, and prevent
China from gaining the officially acknowledged leadership status it seeks
as Asia's undisputed great power.

In addition, operational deployment of Jin class nuclear ballistic
missile submarines based in Hainan began in 2014. It would be surprising
if the PLA Navy did not want to exclude foreign maritime patrol activity
in the South China Sea to protect its nuclear deterrent. The choice of
Hainan as a ballistic missile submarine base is unfortunate because it is
in a small semi-enclosed sea facing unallied states that control the narrow
exits to the blue waters of the Pacific and Indian oceans. Moreover, under
international legal norms any vessel may freely traverse waters beyond
the 12-mile maritime coastal territorial limit, including the world's naval
vessels. Thus, a South China Sea governed by international legal norms
is not well suited to be a secure Chinese naval bastion for nuclear missile

---

[17] Remarks by H.E. Li Keqiang Premier of the State Council of the People's
Republic of China At the 17th ASEAN-China Summit, 13 November 2014. Ibid.

submarines. The desire to turn it into one may explain China's claim of exclusive national jurisdiction within the 9-dash line and the construction of strategically located artificial islands useable for controlling the waters and airspace of the South China Sea.[18]

CHINA'S GREAT POWER AGENDA

China's 2+7 Initiative has to be understood in the context of China's historic drive to achieve great power status. China has the basic requirements of a great power, if this refers to a state whose actions and inactions significantly constrain the choices available to all other states in the world, and whose capabilities permit it to competitively balance against any other state.[19] A great power will tend to have well above average endowments in most if not all of the following areas: GDP, military forces, territory, resources, population, and technological capability. By these criteria, China's rapid progress in GDP, military power, and technological capability have combined with its land, resource, and population endowments to reach the great power threshold.

And yet, the character of a great power inevitably extends beyond possession of material capability to include the desire for international leadership, which is marked by the ability to create or refashion an "international hierarchy of prestige." This ability to create international order refers to the international norms and institutions established by a hegemonic power or a concert of powers that stabilizes and routinizes relations in a society of states that would be unorganized and uncoordinated in its natural state.[20]

---

[18] "China is building a string of artificial islands to fortify its position in the disputed South China Sea", *Business Insider*, 30 January 2015 <http://www.businessinsider.com/china-is-fortifying-position-in-south-china-sea-2015-1>.

[19] Kenneth N. Waltz, *Theory of International Politics* (Reading, MA: Addison-Wesley, 1979).

[20] Robert Gilpin, *War and Change in World Politics* (New York: Cambridge University Press, 1981).

Leadership necessarily entails gaining followers, i.e., states that will join the order sponsored by the leading power(s). The international order set up by a great power will require the use of coercive power and it will reflect its sponsor's interests and values. But it must also satisfy the interests of other states to the extent needed to win their cooperation.[21] And soft power, or the attractiveness of the values and culture of a state, also plays an important role in gaining or alienating potential followers. According to Joseph Nye, a successful great power must be "smart," i.e., it must both satisfy the material interests of followers and appeal to their values and hopes for the future.[22]

China's Campaign for Great Power Status

Many in China saw the Global Financial Crisis of 2008–09 as a strategic opportunity for China to assert itself as an independent great power.[23] Military strategists called it a "new situation marked by major changes in the security environment, in the national interests, and in the balance of power" that called for "new contents, establishing a new line of thinking, and taking new measures."[24] China's neighbours quickly saw more Chinese assertiveness in claiming disputed territories adjoining China's borders, and the West began hearing Chinese criticisms of global governance arrangements. This led Elizabeth C. Economy to comment, "As their economic might expands, they [the Chinese] want not only to assume a greater stake in international organizations but also to remake the rules of the game."[25]

---

[21] John J. Ikenberry, "The Future of International Leadership", *Political Science Quarterly*, Vol. 111, No. 3 (Autumn 1996), pp. 385–402.

[22] Joseph S. Nye, Jr., "Public Diplomacy and Soft Power", *Annals of the American Academy of Political and Social Science*, Vol. 616, Public Diplomacy in a Changing World (Mar., 2008), pp. 94–109.

[23] Wu Xinbo, "Understanding the geopolitical implications of the global financial crisis", *The Washington Quarterly* 33:4 (October 2010), pp. 155–63.

[24] Chen Zhou, "On development of China's defensive national defense policy under the new situation", *Military Science* 6 (2009), pp. 63–71.

[25] Elizabeth C. Economy, "The game changer: Coping with China's foreign policy revolution", *Foreign Affairs*, 89:6 (November/December 2010), p. 143.

However, the fundamental question was whether Deng Xiaoping's strategy of playing along with the U.S. and biding time had outlived its usefulness. Some still advocated, "keeping a low profile". Others favoured "striving for achievement", which called for measured conflict and confrontation in order to create space for Chinese leadership initiatives. This debate broke out during the term of President Hu Jintao (2002–12), who had dedicated China to "peaceful development" and a "harmonious world." It was left to his successor, Xi Jinping, to settle this debate and decide China's path towards great power status. According to Professor Yan Xuetong of Tsinghua University,

> This debate has lasted for years before Chinese President Xi Jinping delivered a speech at the foreign affairs conference of the Chinese Communist Party on October 24, 2013. In this speech, Xi formally presented the strategy of *fenfayouwei* (striving for achievement...), signaling a transformation of China's foreign strategy from the KLP [keeping a low profile] to the SFA [striving for achievement]."[26]

Xi Jinping's Great Power Agenda

Under Xi Jinping's leadership, China is seeking to gain the status of a great power and achieve predominance in Asia. In this sense, Xi Jinping departs from Deng Xiaoping's injunctions to keep a low profile and avoid taking the lead. However, Xi pledges to avoid challenging important US interests outside of Asia and he wishes to avoid a direct military conflict with the U.S.[27] In this sense, he continues to follow Deng's injunctions to bide time and build strength.

The key to understanding China's great power agenda is to look at how Xi envisions and explains China's future. Since coming to power in

---

[26] Yan Xuetong, "From keeping a low profile to striving for achievement", *Chinese Journal of International Politics*, 2014, pp. 153–84.

[27] "Chinese President to Seek New Relationship With U.S. in Talks", *New York Times*, 28 May 2013. <http://www.nytimes.com/2013/05/29/world/asia/china-to-seek-more-equal-footing-with-us-in-talks.html?_r=0>.

2012, Xi Jinping has put forward eight basic concepts that help to define China's diplomatic agenda. Together, they shed light on the ends and means of China's great power agenda. All eight points inform China's new strategy of engagement with ASEAN.

First, the "rejuvenation of the Chinese nation" (中华民族伟大复兴) references recovery from the so-called "century of humiliation" (百年耻辱) that spans China's defeat in the Opium War (1840-42) to the establishment of the People's Republic of China in 1949. The CCP fuels a sense of aggrieved victimhood and a thirst for restored Chinese greatness. The CCP unites all Chinese and gains their support by promising great power status and rectification of past historical injustices.[28]

Second, the "Chinese Dream" (中国梦) means a moderately prosperous society by 2020, and "a modern socialist country that is prosperous, strong, democratic, culturally advanced and harmonious" by 2049. Then, China will re-emerge as a rejuvenated, globally pre-eminent power.[29] The Chinese Dream also involves a selective return to Confucian ethics and values to strengthen national identity and social cohesion under the leadership of the CCP.

Third, China's "core interests" (核心利益) are to defend the legitimacy of the CCP and the state to rule China; the sovereignty and territorial integrity of China; and the stability and development of China's economy.[30] China is committed to peaceful development, but

---

[28] "Xi pledges 'great renewal of the Chinese nation'", Xinhuanet.com, 29 November 2012 <http://news.xinhuanet.com/english/video/2012-11/30/c_132009964.htm>.

[29] "'Chinese Dream' is Xi's vision," *China Daily*, 18 March 2013 <http://www.chinadaily.com.cn/china/2013npc/2013-03/18/content_16315025.htm>; "Xi Jinping's Chinese Dream," *The New York Times*, 4 June 2013 <http://www.nytimes.com/2013/06/05/opinion/global/xi-jinpings-chinese-dream.html>.

[30] In 2009, speaking at the U.S.-China Strategic and Economic Dialogue, State Councilor Dai Bingguo defined China's core interests in the following way: 中国的核心利益第一是维护基本制度和国家安全，其次是国家主权和领土完整，第三是经济社会的持续稳定发展. [首轮中美经济对话:除上月球外主要问题均已谈及, 中国新闻网, 2009年07月29日 09:29 ("First Round of the US-China Economic Dialogue: Other Important Issues Discussed Besides the Moon," *China News Online*, 29 July 2009, 9:29am) <http://www.chinanews.com.cn/gn/news/2009/07-29/1794984.shtml>.

"the principled bottom line" (原则底线) corollary means that China will not sacrifice its core principles to maintain peace. China will use any means at its disposal if its core interests are threatened.[31]

Fourth, the "new type of great power relationship" (新兴大国关系) references a new bilateral relationship with the U.S. marked by the equality of power and status. China's rise has created conflict between China as a rising power and the US as a declining power. Because the prospect of war between the two is unthinkable, Xi Jinping has proposed cooperation based on "mutual respect." The U.S. should respect China's prerogative as Asia's rising great power to reshape Asia. So the United States and its allies in East Asia should "give up cold war thinking," i.e., abandon their alliance relationships that were established in the early stages of the cold war. If the U.S. fails to respect China's interests in this way, the US is accused of trying to "contain" China or obstruct its rise.

Fifth, the "community of common destiny" or "community of shared destiny" (命运共同体) was explicated at a Central Committee work forum on diplomacy towards surrounding countries in October 2013. It was led by Xi Jinping and attended by the entire Politburo Standing Committee, among others.[32] The key ideas or principles that will build the community were listed as follows:

- The use of China's advantages in economy, trade, technology, and finance to build "win-win" cooperation with neighbours;
- Construction of the two Silk Roads;

---

[31] "Xi Jinping Explains the Principled Bottom Line in China's Peaceful Development", *Xinhua Online*, 30 January 2013 (习近平阐明中国和平发展原则底线，新华网，2013年01月30日 <http://www.chinanews.com/gn/2013/01-31/4535125.shtml>.

[32] "Xi Jinping: Let the Sense of Community of Common Destiny Take Deep Root in Neighbouring Countries", Ministry of Foreign Affairs of the People's Republic of China, 25 October 2013 <http://www.fmprc.gov.cn/mfa_chn/zyxw_602251/t1093113.shtml>; "Xi Jinping makes an Important Speech at the Work Forum on Diplomacy toward the Periphery [习近平在周边外交工作座谈会上发表重要讲话]," *Xinhua*, 25 October 2013 <http://www.chinanews.com/gn/2013/10-25/5427062.shtml>.

- The use of trade and investment to create a new kind of regional economic integration;
- An AIIB, internationalization of the RMB, and regional financial stability;
- The development of Chinese border areas as gateways to neighbouring countries;
- A new concept of security, based on mutual trust, reciprocity, equality, and coordination through enhanced cooperation mechanisms.
- Public diplomacy and people-to-people exchanges including tourism, technology, education, and provincial level cooperation.[33]

The West's favoured approach to regional integration (e.g., NAFTA and the EU) is economic liberalization. This uses multilateral treaties to remove legal and institutional barriers to trade and investment, and it creates uniform rules, standards, and dispute resolution mechanisms that states must follow to create a flat open playing field freely accessible to private sector activity. It does not focus on the provision of physical infrastructure or the channeling of trade to serve a particular national interest; the direction of trade and investment is left for the free market to determine.

In contrast, China's approach to regional integration centres on policy-led trade facilitation. This features the improvement of trade connectivity by building more efficient transportation linkages, providing more trade and investment finance, streamlining trade and investment approvals, and multiplying human exchange opportunities. It requires policy dialogue between states to shape the direction of development rather than the

---

[33] "Xi Jinping: Let the Sense of Community of Common Destiny Take Deep Root in Neighbouring Countries," Ministry of Foreign Affairs of the People's Republic of China, 25 October 2013 <http://www.fmprc.gov.cn/mfa_chn/zyxw_602251/t1093113.shtml>; This agenda was reaffirmed in a broader and more confident vision of Chinese great power leadership at a Central Work Meeting on Foreign Affairs in November 2014. See 习近平出席中央外事工作会议并发表重要发表 ("Xi Jinping attends the Central Work Meeting on Foreign Affairs to make an important speech,") *Xinhua Online*, 29 November 2014 <http://news.xinhuanet.com/politics/2014-11/29/c_1113457723.htm>.

adoption of uniform and legally binding rules that give private sector actors freedom to allocate resources.

China's policy dialogues will be managed in hub-and-spoke fashion according to the principle of "reciprocity." That is, cooperation with China will be rewarded, and non-cooperation will have negative consequences. China does not intend to create supranational institutions or legally binding multilateral treaties to create a self-governing community of states. It wants a community of states dependent on China's superior wealth, power, and strategic centrality.

Sixth, the "New Silk Road Economic Belt" (丝绸之路经济带) and the "21st Century Maritime Silk Road" (21世纪海上丝绸之路) initiatives were announced by Xi Jinping in September and October 2013 respectively. The combined silk roads agenda, the so-called "One Belt-One Road" (一带 一路) programme, is intended to create economic connectivity to sustain China's continuing growth, and to make the economic prosperity of surrounding regions dependent on China's growth.[34] The construction of physical transportation infrastructure financed by new development banks and other sources of investment will pave the way for Chinese trade, private investment, monetary cooperation, tourism, and cultural exchange across Eurasia.[35] Because of the vast difference in economic scale between China and its neighbours, deepening economic interdependence will give China leverage to set rules and expectation for others to follow. The countries along the two silk roads are expected to join China's community of common destiny.

Seventh, the New Asian Security Concept was introduced by Xi Jinping at the Conference on Interaction and Confidence Building Measures in Asia (CICA) summit in May 2014.[36] CICA is an obscure

---

[34] "Xi's Strategic Conception of 'One Belt and One Road' Has Great Significance," CRIEnglish.com, 11 October 2014 <http://english.cri.cn/12394/2014/10/11/53s847421.htm>.

[35] Zhu Feng."New Silk Road Economic Belt-Spearhead of China's Westward Strategy" *China Daily*, 3 December 2013 <http://www.chinatoday.com.cn/english/report/2013-12/03/content_581254.htm>.

[36] "Statement by H.E. Mr. Xi Jinping", Conference on Interaction and Confidence Building Measures In Asia, 21 May 2014 <http://www.s-cica.org/page.php?page_id=711&lang=1>.

security discussion forum created by Kazakhstan that features Eurasian membership. Japan and NATO members are conspicuously absent. According to President Xi, "it is for the people of Asia to run the affairs of Asia, solve the problems of Asia, and uphold the security of Asia." Security in Asia centers on development, and China sees no role for traditional alliances or legally binding multilateral security commitments. Instead, informal regional discussion of broad comprehensive security concerns is desired. In the absence of a legally binding multilateral regional security regime or alliances between states, a powerful China would be relatively unconstrained when dealing with smaller neighbouring countries.

Finally, the international rule of law as understood by China informs its international behaviour. International law as developed under the Westphalian international order is meant not only to create sovereign state authority, but also to act as a brake on the arbitrary exercise of state power, and to create an international community of states with agreed norms and procedures for peacefully managing their relations.

In explaining China's understanding of the international rule of law, Foreign Minister Wang Yi stated: "Such principles as respect for sovereignty and territorial integrity, peaceful settlement of international disputes and non-interference in the internal affairs of others, as enshrined in the UN Charter, are the foundation stones upon which modern international law and conduct of international relations are built."[37] This definition omits core legal norms in the UN Charter such as state accountability to law, respect for human rights, and the resort to independent adjudication of disputes.[38] These are the core principles of

---

[37] "Full text of Chinese FM's signed article on int'l rule of law," *Xinhua*, 24 October 2014 <http://en.people.cn/n/2014/1024/c90883-8799769-2.html>.

[38] The UN's definition of the international rule of law starts off this way: "a principle of governance in which all persons, institutions and entities, public and private, *including the State itself*, are accountable to laws that are publicly promulgated, equally enforced and *independently adjudicated*, and which are consistent with *international human rights norms and standards* ..." (italics added). *What is the rule of law?* United Nations Rule of Law website <http://www.unrol.org/article.aspx?article_id=3>.

the international rule of law that limit arbitrary state power and create a law-governed community of state.

With respect to international judicial institutions, Wang Yi warned: "[they] should avoid overstepping their authority... Still less should they encroach on the rights and interests of other countries under the pretext of 'the rule of law' in total disregard of objectivity and fairness." This begs the question, who will apply international law with objectivity and fairness when China's interests conflict with those of its neighbours?

The answer is found in China's diplomatic practice. As demonstrated by its words and actions in its East China Sea and South China Sea disputes, China does not turn to impartial international tribunals to resolve jurisdictional disputes. Instead, it insists on direct bilateral negotiations with individual disputants, warns that it will not compromise over "core interests", and holds in reserve the "principled bottom line." At the Politburo group study session on 29 January 2013, Xi Jinping stated, "No country should presume that we will engage in trade involving our core interests or that we will swallow the 'bitter fruit' of harming our sovereignty, security or development interests."[39] This maximizes China's power advantage in bilateral negotiation and it excludes impartial third-party adjudication that would ensure fairness in the application of law.

The implications of China's idiosyncratic understanding of the international rule of law, combined with reciprocity diplomacy and the principled bottom line, are that smaller countries will lack the protection of the full range of international legal norms and institutions when disputing China. They will need to accommodate themselves to Chinese power in order to avoid the loss of rights and privileges in the community of common destiny.

Together, these eight concepts point to a China-centric regional sphere that will differ from the existing liberal global order. China's

---

[39] "Xi Jinping Explains the Principled Bottom Line in China's Peaceful Development", *Xinhua Online*, 30 January 2013 (习近平阐明中国和平发展原则底线，新华网，2013年01月30日) <http://www.chinanews.com/gn/2013/01-31/4535125.shtml>; "China's development to remain peaceful: Xi", *Xinhuanet*, 29 January 2013 <http://news.xinhuanet.com/english/china/2013-01/29/c_132135826.htm>.

great power agenda does not seek to uproot and replace the entire liberal international order. It works to displace it in Asia by establishing China as the natural leader or core power in an Asian community of common destiny that operates according to a different set of principles, norms, and institutional procedures.

This approach to regional order is different from ASEAN-style community in important respects. The core-periphery structure of connectivity, governance, and membership in China's community of shared destiny differs from the kind of non-coercive, equal, and impartial multilateralism that ASEAN has developed.

ASEAN'S INSTITUTIONAL DILEMMAS

China's Southeast Asian neighbours are logical prospects for early recruitment into China's Community of Common Destiny. They are not only close and easily accessible; they are also much smaller and more easily dominated than other countries that border China. None hosts a large U.S. military presence,[40] and none falls within a sphere of influence claimed by a neighbouring major power such as Russia, India, or Japan. They are also conveniently organized as a group in ASEAN, making it easy for China to collectively engage them. Cultivating habits of collective ASEAN followership and deference to China helps to secure Beijing's South China Sea ambitions and great power aspirations.

ASEAN's value to its members resides in its ability to attract and hold the attention of more powerful external actors, which ASEAN members would never do if they acted independently. Its members locate a lowest common denominator of shared national interest, and trade on this with larger external actors to gain shared benefits. This was not difficult to do when ASEAN asked for little more than inclusive and informal discussions about Southeast Asian security and trade facilitation with larger external powers.

---

[40] The U.S. withdrew its forces and base presence from Thailand in 1976 and from the Philippines in 1992.

But the game changes if ASEAN thinks that a formal charter and stronger rules will allow it to negotiate more substantive agreements with external powers. Negotiation with an external power can be difficult for a diverse collection of small states to manage. And because any agreement will generate costs and benefits that will be unevenly distributed among members, ASEAN must pay attention to distributional justice or risk internal unity.

China offers ASEAN substantial economic benefits and in return, China expects ASEAN to endorse China's economic, political, and security leadership agendas. But the distribution of benefits in these different dimensions is uneven. Vietnam and the Philippines have not been offered the multi-billion dollar port and railway development projects offered to Myanmar, Thailand, Laos, Cambodia, Malaysia, and Indonesia. Moreover, these big projects could create diminished opportunity for those left out. A new port and railway in one country may draw trade, investment, and growth from a neighbour, leaving that neighbour's economic prospects worse off than before.

In political-security areas the costs and benefits also fall unevenly within ASEAN. A summit meeting with a Chinese leader and expensive new national projects are of great political value to ASEAN members that face western criticism in human rights matters. At the same time, China's 2+7 initiative can damage the political and security interests of others. Vietnam and the Philippines are losers if their conflicts with China are side-tracked and ignored by ASEAN.

Perhaps it is only coincidental that Vietnam and the Philippines, two ASEAN members whose territorial and maritime jurisdictional claims overlap those of China, and who actively resist China's unilateral efforts to change the status quo, face losses in the political-security dimension and are left out of big economic benefits from China's 2+7 Initiative. ASEAN can entertain an external power's offer of unequal tradeoffs and divide and rule strategems so long as ASEAN can uphold the lowest common denominator principle. That is, benefits can be unevenly distributed, but ASEAN should never agree to something that leaves a member significantly worse off than before. There are three basic strategems that ASEAN can flexibly deploy to defend this principle as circumstances require.

First, ASEAN can untie or disaggregate a complex package of agreements and undertakings and negotiate each component item separately. This can be effective in the case of the 2+7 Initiative because the economic benefits that China offers, e.g., a port investment or railway projects, tend to serve China's own interests as much as the intended recipients' interests. And untying these economic benefits from the political-security agenda allows China's requests for concessions in political and security issues to be considered apart from monetary considerations.

Second, in theory, winners could compensate losers to make an external agreement work, though in practice this may be difficult for ASEAN to manage.

Finally, ASEAN should announce that it cannot agree to undertakings that significantly damage the national interest of a member country. This creates ASEAN bargaining leverage and warns off external powers from attempting divide-and-rule diplomatic manoeuvres.

CONCLUSION

ASEAN has difficulty in negotiating with a powerful China that thinks strategically and acts quickly. This makes it all the more important for ASEAN to have worked out bottom line principles before an external power approaches with a substantive proposal to cooperatively manage Southeast Asian economic, political, and security affairs. ASEAN cannot become a mechanism used by some members to gain benefits at the expense of other members and still remain true to its original purpose. Based on a lowest common denominator principle of unity and solidarity, ASEAN can respond to complex package offers by unwrapping the package and selecting only the items that benefit—and do not harm—its members, and by declaring that ASEAN will not collectively agree to undertakings that undermine the national interest of any member.

In the longer term, China's 2+7 Initiative aims to help China achieve great power status and a China-centred order in Eurasia by bringing Southeast Asia into deeper relations of economic, political, and security dependence on China. While no formal treaty relating to participation in a China-centred community of common destiny may ever obstruct a member's choice of economic, political, and strategic relations, according to the design of a China-centred community of common destiny, members can face bilaterally administered disciplines that will have the same effect. Therefore, ASEAN should continue to pursue balanced relations with external powers, and take steps to maintain ASEAN's centrality in managing Southeast Asian affairs.